SARA USES HER WORDS WISELY

Dalia Ramzi Mohammad

Editor: Noor Hammoud
Copyright ©2019 by Dalia Ramzi Mohammad

Riiing! The recess bell chimed.
Sara ran outside with her classmates
to play jump rope.
Everyone was excited.

Just then, her friend Maya asked
if she wanted to play ball instead.
She was excited to jump rope but
didn't want to hurt Maya's feelings.
Sara remembered that Allah
loves us to tell the truth,
but to do so in a nice way.
She replied, "Thank you for asking me,
but I feel like jump roping right now."
Maya smiled and said,
"Okay, maybe next time."

As Sara waited, she saw
her friend Ranya cut in line.
Sara felt that this was not fair
for everyone else in line.
Even though Ranya was her friend,
she remembered that Allah
reminds us to stand up for what's right.
So Sara decided to speak up,
"Ranya, did you realize that you cut in line?"
Ranya responded, "I did. I'm sorry."
She then made her way to the back of the line.

As Sara continued
to wait her turn
she heard some girls
whispering behind her,
"Look at Nada, she jumps funny."
They began to giggle.

Sara did not want anyone to say anything mean about Nada.
She knew that Allah does not like it when we speak badly of others.
Sara bravely said,
"I am so proud of her! Look at her go!"
The girls knew better than to speak badly.
They stopped and cheered for Nada.

When Sara finished jump roping,
she remembered that she promised
Mila that she would play with her.
Sara thought about how Allah
tells us to keep our promises.
So, Sara decided to run over to Mila,
"Let's go play together!"
They ran excitedly together
to the seesaw and had a lot of fun.

As Sara walked back to school,
she felt good about the way
she used her words.
Speaking the truth,
standing up for what's right,
and keeping promises are all qualities
that make Allah happy with us
and make us happy with ourselves.

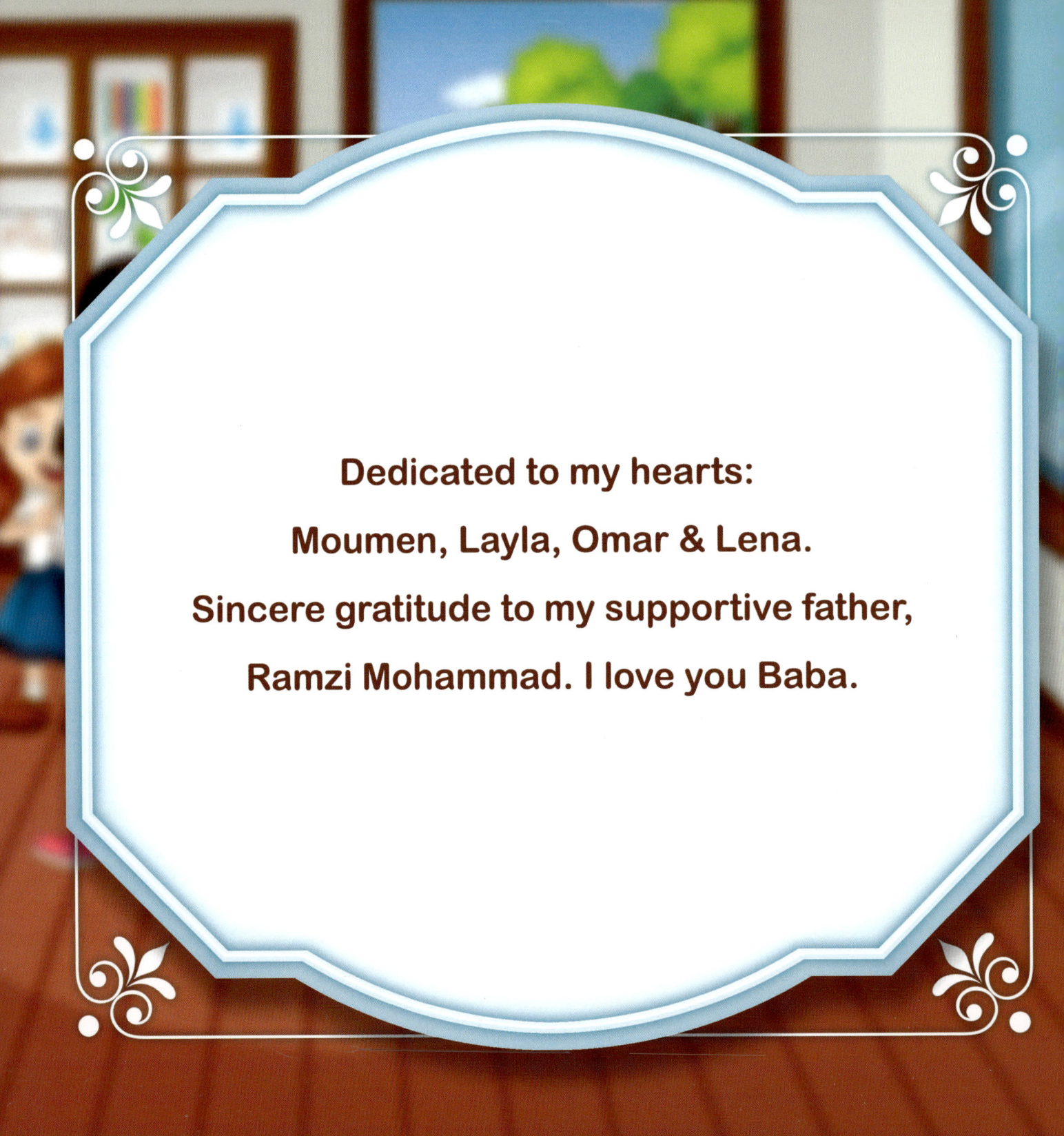

Dedicated to my hearts:

Moumen, Layla, Omar & Lena.

Sincere gratitude to my supportive father,

Ramzi Mohammad. I love you Baba.